I Am Every Woman

AN IN-DEPTH STUDY
OF WOMEN IN THE BIBLE

SANDY A. STOVALL

WESTBOW
PRESS®
A DIVISION OF THOMAS NELSON
& ZONDERVAN

Copyright © 2022 Sandy A. Stovall.

All rights reserved. No part of this book may be used or reproduced by any means, graphic, electronic, or mechanical, including photocopying, recording, taping or by any information storage retrieval system without the written permission of the author except in the case of brief quotations embodied in critical articles and reviews.

WestBow Press books may be ordered through booksellers or by contacting:

WestBow Press
A Division of Thomas Nelson & Zondervan
1663 Liberty Drive
Bloomington, IN 47403
www.westbowpress.com
844-714-3454

Because of the dynamic nature of the Internet, any web addresses or links contained in this book may have changed since publication and may no longer be valid. The views expressed in this work are solely those of the author and do not necessarily reflect the views of the publisher, and the publisher hereby disclaims any responsibility for them.

Any people depicted in stock imagery provided by Getty Images are models, and such images are being used for illustrative purposes only. Certain stock imagery © Getty Images.

Scripture quotations marked HCSB are taken from the Holman Christian Standard Bible®, Copyright © 1999, 2000, 2002, 2003, 2009 by Holman Bible Publishers. Used by permission. Holman Christian Standard Bible®, Holman CSB®, and HCSB® are federally registered trademarks of Holman Bible Publishers.

Scripture quotations taken from the (NASB®) New American Standard Bible®, Copyright © 1960, 1971, 1977, 1995, 2020 by The Lockman Foundation. Used by permission. All rights reserved. www.lockman.org

Scripture taken from the New King James Version® Copyright © 1982 by Thomas Nelson. Used by permission. All rights reserved.

ISBN: 978-1-6642-7194-4 (sc)
ISBN: 978-1-6642-7196-8 (hc)
ISBN: 978-1-6642-7195-1 (e)

Library of Congress Control Number: 2022912701

Print information available on the last page.

WestBow Press rev. date: 8/12/2022

Contents

1. Believing It before It Is Done 1
2. When God Calls Your Name 15
3. Lies, Loyalty, and Death 29
4. God's Plan Will Always Prevail 41
5. Obedience Pays Off 51
6. Seeking Justice, Give Us What We Deserve 63
7. Wearing Wisdom Well 77
8. A Selfless Act 89
9. A Lustful Heart 103
10. A Longing Desire 117
11. The Avenger 127
12. The Power of Paganism: Solomon's Pagan Wives 139

Encouraging Words 151

Thank You, Holy Spirit, for Your guidance in writing, *I'm Every Woman!* To my husband, Wendell, thank you for your unwavering support. To my daughters, Neca, Dyneshia, Keshia, and Mauri, thank you for always supporting me. You all are the best!

Chapter One
BELIEVING IT BEFORE IT IS DONE

The Shunammite Woman
2 KINGS 4:20-24 (NKJV)

[20]When he had taken him and brought him to his mother, he sat on her knees till noon and then died. [21]And she went up and laid him on the bed of the man of God, shut the door upon him, and went out. [22]Then she called to her husband, and said, "Please send me one of the young men and one of the donkeys that I may run to the man of God and come back." [23]So he said, "Why are you going to him today? It is neither the New Moon nor the Sabbath." And she said, "It is well." [24]Then she saddled a donkey, and said to her servant, "Drive, and go forward; do not slacken the pace for me unless I tell you."

Her Story

The Shunammite woman was a mother, wife, believer, and servant of God. She was a prominent woman in Shunem, a place the prophet Elisha visited often. Whenever he passed through Shunem, she would encourage him to eat with her. The Shunammite woman showed her servanthood through her actions. Because Elisha traveled that way often, she decided to make her husband aware of whom they were caring for. "I know that the one who often passes by here is a holy man of God" (2 Kings 4:9 HCSB). Then, in all her wisdom, she politely asked her husband if they could set up a room for Elisha in their home.

> What are some of your roles as a woman?

> How do these roles affect your service to God?

Because of her generosity and compassion, Elisha thanked her and asked what he could do in exchange. She did not want anything. Gehazi, Elisha's servant, spoke up and said she did not have a son. Elisha then proclaimed a blessing upon her. "At this time next year, you will have a son in your arms" (2 Kings 4:16 HCSB). Just as the prophet spoke, she conceived and gave birth.

> Do your generosity and compassion warrant blessings? What do you expect God to do for you?

Her son grew into a young man and became ill. Her husband brought their son to her. He sat on her lap and died. She activated her faith by carrying her son's body to Elisha's bed to lay him there while she set out to find Elisha and bring him back to help her.

The Shunammite woman made it to Mount Carmel, fell at Elisha's feet, and said she was not leaving without him. So, they proceeded to her home together.

When Elisha arrived, the boy's body was lying on his bed. Elisha shut the door after entering the room and prayed to God. Then he laid on the boy, put his mouth on his mouth, his eyes on his eyes, and his hands on his hands, and stretched out over the boy. It was not until Elisha performed these actions that the boy's flesh started feeling warm. He got up, walked back and forth in the house, and stretched out over him again. This time, the boy sneezed seven times and then opened his eyes. When the boy opened his eyes, Elisha called Gehazi and told him to tell the Shunammite woman to come to get her son.

Precisely what she believed God would do happened. Never

did she doubt the power of God. Never did she waver in her faith. On the contrary, she spoke, believed, and acted upon her faith. Because of her ability to believe God for the impossible, her son rose from the dead. Taking a leap of faith in any situation can be scary sometimes.

> What do you want God to do in your life that requires you to take a leap of faith?

Application

When the Shunammite's son died in her arms, she responded by stating, "It is well" (2 Kings 4:23 NKJV). Even after seeing her son dead, she still believed everything would work out. She showed her belief in the power of God through her response. How could she have known her son would live again? I do not know. But based on her reaction, she believed God's prophet would be able to help her.

Can you look beyond your troubles and see victory?

Believing God beyond what you can see can be difficult. So, what is keeping you from seeing victory?

> And she went up and laid him on the bed of the man of God. (2 Kings 4:21 NKJV)
>
> **Faith Move #1:** After he died, she *laid* him on the bed—not just any bed but Elisha's bed, the man of God.

Whenever we lay something down, we are placing it in a position of rest. The Shunammite woman knew her son was dead, but she acted as if he were asleep. She refused to accept the outcome that was right before her. Many times, we do not allow our faith to go beyond what we see. We believe, but only as far as our senses will allow.

> Is there a dead situation God needs to revive in your life?

Her next faith move was even more powerful than the first. "Please send me one of the young men and one of the donkeys, that I may run to the man of God and come back" (2 Kings 4:22 NKJV).

> **Faith Move #2:** She said, "That I may *run* to the man of God and come back" (2 Kings 4:22 NKJV, emphasis added).

There was a sense of urgency in her quest to get to Elisha. She did not have time to waste. We see this urgency when she said to her servant, "Drive and go forward; do not slacken the pace for me unless I tell you" (2 Kings 4:24 NKJV). In other words, I need to hurry and get to the man of God.

> Is there anything in your life that would cause you to seek God urgently? Why or why not?

We should be in a hurry to seek after God, just as the Shunammite woman was. For her, it was a life-and-death situation.

> Describe a life and death situation that would cause you to seek after God hurriedly.

We are always in a hurry. This is our pattern when it comes to living life.

However, when handling God's business, we are slow to move until we are faced with tragedy. Then, the sad part is, we will commit to doing everything other than serving God consistently.

The Shunammite woman's pattern was serving the man of God, making him comfortable *every* time he passed through her city. She was consistent in her quest to honor him because honoring Elisha meant she was glorifying God.

We are not consistent when it comes to serving God. Instead, we are procrastinative, unbothered, and determined to take care of *our* business.

> Why do you think this is?

She laid her son in a temporary resting place, not a permanent one. She did not follow the customary ritual of burying the dead. Her faith told her he was in a temporary state of rest.

| Identify a bad situation in your life, past or present. Do you think it was permanent or temporary? How did you handle it?

| What do you believe God can accomplish that may seem impossible?

> What action(s) would you take to show you have faith that God can do the impossible?

We will believe God initially, but when death comes upon that situation, our faith starts wavering. We will believe Him while sickness is reigning prevalent through the body, but we waver when it goes beyond that. We say He can make all things work together for our good, but our actions say differently.

My Testimony

I was in my early thirties, living life to the fullest when I was hit with a scare. I found a lump in my left breast. The doctor said they wanted to perform a biopsy to see if it was benign or malignant. Just hearing the words *benign* and *malignant* activated emotions I thought were gone! At that moment, all I could think about was *cancer*. Soon after the paralyzing thoughts invaded my mind, I gathered myself, shifted my focus, and called on my Healer, God. Unfortunately, my appointment was not scheduled for another three weeks. So, I had twenty-one days for my mind to be engulfed with negative thoughts.

Instead of remaining in that state, I redirected my thoughts to the Word of God and His healing power. I began claiming my healing long before the biopsy took place. I knew God was the Healer, and no doctor could top that. Although I was still a tad bit nervous, I did not let it consume me. I chose victory over being a victim. I fasted and prayed, believing in and thanking God for what He was getting ready to do in my life.

If I were to be diagnosed with cancer, I had already made up my mind that God would heal me. I never spoke a negative word about my situation. All I could do was claim the victory I knew was imminent. Finally, it was time. Three weeks had come and gone. I arrived at Park Plaza outpatient clinic early that morning with my brother, Bruce. He was my natural supporter, while God was my spiritual Supporter.

As I was transported to surgery, I felt a sense of relief. I knew God had heard my prayers. Therefore, I spoke, saw, and believed my results were *already* benign. I was not accepting anything less. My God is a Healer, and I went into the operating room with that mindset. The procedure went well. When I woke up, the doctor came into my hospital room and said they had removed the lump. It was a benign tumor. No cancer! Tears of joy began rolling down my face. I started thanking God. I believed my faith made me whole. Even if it had been cancer, I knew—without a shadow of a doubt—that God could heal me. Just as the Shunammite woman knew the man of God could raise her son from the dead because of the power of God that flowed through Elisha, I knew that same power flowed through me, and my God would heal my body.

Trusting, believing, and walking as though it is finished shows your faith. Just from those three words, *"It is well"* (2 Kings 4:23 NKJV, emphasis added), the Shunammite woman exhibited her faith before God raised her son. She put action to what she believed in her heart, and so did I.

Prayer

Father God, I stand before You with a willing heart and a humble spirit, giving You all the praise and glory. Knowing that all I must do is believe in my heart, speak Your word, and act upon what I know You can and will do, gives me the confidence I need to keep pressing forward. It does not matter what I face; I will look beyond my problems and see You. I will no longer see any situation as a lost cause. Instead, I will see everything as an opportunity for You to show up. Just as the Shunammite woman knew You would raise her son from the dead, I understand that any seemingly dead situation I face, You can give it life. Thank You for never failing me. Thank You for releasing Your power upon me, my life, and everything I will face. It is in Your Son, Jesus's name I pray, amen!

Notes

Chapter Two
WHEN GOD CALLS YOUR NAME

Dorcas (Tabitha)
ACTS 9:36–42 (NASB)

³⁶ Now in Joppa there was a disciple named Tabitha (translated in Greek the name is Dorcas); this woman was abounding with deeds of kindness and charity, which she continually did. ³⁷And it happened at that time that she fell sick and died and when they had washed her body, they laid it in an upper room. ³⁸Since Lydda was near Joppa, the disciples, having heard that Peter was there, sent two men to him, imploring him, "Do not delay in coming to us." ³⁹So Peter arose and went with them. When he arrived, they brought him into the upper room; and all the widows stood beside him weeping and showing all the tunics and garments that Dorcas used to make while she was with them. ⁴⁰But Peter sent them all out and knelt down and prayed, and turning to the body, he said, "Tabitha, arise." And she opened her eyes, and when she saw Peter, she sat up. ⁴¹And he gave her his hand and raised her up; and calling the saints and widows, he presented her alive. ⁴²It became known all over Joppa, and many believed in the Lord.

Her Story

Dorcas was a well-known disciple throughout Joppa. Her name means *gazelle*, which is a beautiful, graceful creature. Her inner beauty was exhibited through her outward actions: charity, compassion, love, and kindness. She was the epitome of a selfless, faithful servant who gave herself to the work of the Lord by helping the widows and others in her community.

> What characteristics do you possess that would draw people to you?

> Is it challenging to maintain those attributes throughout your life? Why or why not?

Your lifestyle is an accurate representation of who you are on the inside. Take a good look at yourself.

> Who or what do you see?

One day Dorcas became very sick and died. This was a tragic occurrence for all those who knew her. Immediately upon her death, those around her sought after Peter, who was in the town of Lydda, about eleven miles away.

When Peter arrived, he walked in on the grief-stricken women sobbing profusely for Dorcas. The tunics and garments Dorcas had made were all they had left.

Peter saw their pain but knew he had work to do. After sending them out of the room, he knelt and prayed. Peter turned toward Dorcas's dead body and called her name. "Tabitha arise!" (Acts 9:40 NASB) No longer a lifeless body, she caught sight of Peter and sat up. (Reminder that *Tabitha* is Hebrew for *Dorcas*.)

Gently placing her hand in his, he helped her to her feet, opened the door, and presented her to all those waiting in the other room. God had miraculously come through, and it was known throughout Joppa.

Many times, it takes a miracle to get the attention of others. However, God is in the business of drawing people to Himself, and He will do whatever needs to be done to get their attention.

Has God had to use extreme measures to get your attention? Explain.

Application

Dorcas was a devoted disciple full of good works and acts of charity. She gave to the needy. Giving must come from the heart. It cannot be conditional. When giving emerges from the heart, nothing is expected in return. That was Dorcas. Serving unconditionally was what she chose to do.

Serving others and serving yourself is critical. One cannot outweigh the other because both are needed. We must learn to balance our lives in a way that will yield satisfaction in all areas.

> List some of the ways you have served others and yourself. I have listed two examples.

Serving Others	Serving Ourselves
Listen attentively, without interruptions.	Allow time for mental rest.

What are some good works and acts of charity you've contributed throughout your life?

Tell a story of how you serve others in the box below.

Widows and other saints benefited greatly from Dorcas's kindness. Sometimes we do things out of obligation or because it is just the right thing to do. Dorcas served out of love and compassion for others. The tunics and garments she made were evidence and a reminder of her charity and good works.

> Who has benefited from your or others' good works and acts of charity? What evidence can be shown of this?

> If you were the one serving, what were your reasons for performing these acts? (someone asked you to do it, volunteered, the right thing to do, forced, etc.) Describe how you felt.

> Did you expect anything in return? Why or why not?

Dorcas left a lasting impact on others by consistently doing good works and acts of charity.

> Discuss a time someone impacted your life.

Ironically, they washed Dorcas's body and laid it in the upper room. There was no rush to bury her. Their actions displayed their faith. Faith told them not to entomb her. They held her there and summoned the man of God, who could seek Jesus on behalf of their dearly beloved. Their hope in the power of Christ was astounding.

> Do you have enough faith to seek God on behalf of someone else? Are you in a position to intercede on behalf of others? Explain.

Before Dorcas could be raised from the dead, all distractions had to be removed.

Sometimes we cannot tap into the power of God because of the distractions. God wants our undivided attention. To hear Him clearly, silence is needed. Distractions will always keep you from operating in the full power of the Spirit.

There are many distractions around us, causing chaos and confusion. They keep us busy so that we won't be able to focus on the task at hand. We must be able to hear clearly when doing the work of God.

He gives us specific assignments to carry out, and if we are not in a place where we can hone in on His voice, we can miss our opportunity to achieve the task at hand.

> What's keeping you from tapping into the unlimited power of Jesus? List your distractions.

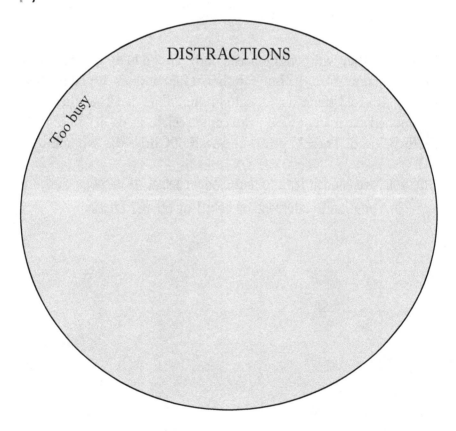

> Do you find it easy or difficult to remove all distractions? Why or why not?

We must remove all distractions if we are going to hear from God. Prayer was Peter's very next step after he removed the distractions. Concentration and meditation are needed when seeking to tap into the power of the living God. We can only do this when we are alone, and our thoughts are undisturbed.

Dorcas's resurrection showed the power of God in a way that could never be denied. When the power of Jesus awakens a dead situation, you cannot help but get up and get moving. God's power will not allow you to remain in a dead state. So when God calls your name, you will rise out of that lifeless situation and proceed forward.

> Talk about a time in your life or in the life of someone close to you where you thought a situation or relationship was dead, only to be resurrected later.

My Testimony

God called me out of the darkness at the tender age of twelve. For one year, it was all about God, the Bible, and the church. I was focused on the word of God and being obedient to all that I learned. I was on fire for Him and wanted the entire world to know.

Fast-forward to age thirteen. I backslid! That's right; I was no longer saved, at least that's what I thought. But I knew the Bible said, in Jeremiah 3:14, "Return, O backsliding children, says the Lord; for I am married to you" (NKJV).

But that did not matter to me. I felt as though I had messed up, and since I convinced myself that it was over, I lived accordingly. My salvation was dead as far as I was concerned. I found myself in a whirlwind of trouble, rebellion, revenge, hatred, unforgiveness, and much more. My life was spiraling out of control. Therefore, I had no desire to remain on this earth.

I felt dead inside. I was depressed, alone, and unloved. I hated who I had become. So I concocted a plan to handle it by becoming the invisible thirteen year old no one saw anyway. Unfortunately, it seemed as if I was invisible to the one person who meant the most to me, my mother. At that point, I began despising the woman who had birthed me into this world. I had reached my breaking point of no return. If she did not want me, why live?

God had a different plan for me because, after my unprecedented act, I called my grandmother and told her what I was dealing with. She immediately started praying. Her words were, "Devil, you cannot have my granddaughter! Satan, the Lord rebukes you! Baby, it is going to be okay. God has a great work for you, and the enemy wants to destroy you. But He cannot have you."

From that day forward, I felt as though God had cleansed me. He purged, purified, and renewed me. I wept some more, but this time I was praising and thanking God for deliverance.

In my mind and heart, my life was over. But God was not done with me. God used Peter to render life back into Dorcas's dead body, raise her, and present her alive to all the people in her town, and He did the same for me.

Do not ever discount the power of Jesus. He can raise us from any dead state if He chooses. Life does not end until God says it is over!

Prayer

Father God, I come boldly before You, giving You honor, praise, and glory. Lord, I've found myself in many dead situations, feeling as though I was irrelevant. I felt all hope was gone, and my life had come to an end. Lord, I surrender these vague feelings to You. I no longer want to embrace irrelevancy. I want to feel as though You have a purpose for me. I know You have one, but I need that feeling to resonate in my heart. Use me to bring life to those who have felt just like me. Allow me to share the everlasting life You have given me with others. Teach me how not to fall prey to the attacks of the enemy. Protect me from any and every dead situation that may arise. Thank You for renewing my heart and mind. Thank You for giving me another chance to get it right. Thank You for forgiving me for all the times I tried to eradicate myself from this earth, directly or indirectly. It is in Your Son, Jesus's name I pray, amen!

Chapter Three
LIES, LOYALTY, AND DEATH

Sapphira
ACTS 5:7–11 (NASB)

⁷Now there elapsed an interval of about three hours, and his wife came in, not knowing what had happened. ⁸And Peter responded to her, "Tell me whether you sold the land for such and such a price?" And she said, "Yes, that was the price." ⁹Then Peter said to her, "Why is it that you have agreed together to put the Spirit of the Lord to the test? Behold, the feet of those who have buried your husband are at the door, and they will carry you out as well." ¹⁰And immediately she fell at his feet and breathed her last, and the young men came in and found her dead, and they carried her out and buried her beside her husband. ¹¹And great fear came over the whole church, and over all who heard of these things.

Her Story

Sapphira's husband, Ananias, sold property and decided to keep some of the money from the sale. Sapphira was fully aware of his actions, and she still supported his decision. This showed her unyielding allegiance to the man she loved. Whether or not she knew, the consequences of participating in such a deceitful scheme did not matter. This is the real danger of being loyal beyond a lie. It could cost you a great deal. Her loyalty to Ananias was more important than standing for the truth. This was demonstrated by her willingness to uphold the plan.

> Have you ever supported someone you knew was wrong, but you stood by them anyway because of the love?

> What were the consequences of you supporting them?

Sapphira's story is an intriguing one. It reveals a loyalty that caused her life to end in tragedy. Many women have found themselves in the same position as Sapphira. They support the men in their lives, only to find out the choice they made did more harm than good. The damage was done, and there was no turning back.

> Examine your loyalty to others. What could it possibly cost you, good or bad?

Sapphira decided to support her husband, which meant she had to keep lying about the money. She probably thought she would get away with deceiving Peter. Once she appeared before Peter, there was no turning back. Her loyalty to her husband prevailed.

> Think about a time you lied and thought no one knew. Describe how you would feel if that lie or lies were exposed so all could see.

Three hours later, without the knowledge of what just occurred, the death of her husband, she stood before Peter to answer questions about the sale of their land. He specifically asked her if the land had sold for a specific price. Without hesitation, she said yes.

To Peter's astonishment, another lie was told. He asked why she had agreed to go along with this scheme and test the Holy Spirit. Because she lied, he let her know that the same men who had carried her husband's body out would come and do the same to hers. Immediately she fell dead, just as Ananias had. Both were untruthful. However, Sapphira had been given an opportunity to tell the truth, and she'd failed to do so. Her loyalty rested solely with her husband and not God. Because she'd chosen her loyalty to Ananias over God, death was the ultimate price. Sometimes our actions will bring about an unexpected outcome. Many times, when a specific question is asked, you can rest assured the answer is already known.

> How often have you asked someone a question and already knew the answer?

| Was the truth or a lie exposed? What was the outcome?

| Have you ever found yourself displaying misplaced loyalty to someone you love? If not, do you know someone who has? Is it easily identifiable? Explain.

Misplaced loyalty can compel you to walk into a situation blindly, not knowing the consequences that can arise. The price you may have to pay could be more than you could ever imagine. When you are loyal to someone who lies and is deceitful, the result could be fatal.

For example, say your friend commits a crime, and you know exactly what this person has done. But you choose to provide an alibi or support him. Because of your loyalty, you have subjected yourself to dire consequences. Now, you have placed yourself in a position to receive punishment from the law, by being guilty by association. Most importantly, you lied, and it could cost you your freedom.

How many opportunities have God given you to tell the truth? Did you pass or fail?

Write the details of your success or failure.

Application

Sapphira's devotion to her husband led her to a shocking end. This is the ultimate hindrance because progression is no longer an option. Death is a permanent end.

List the people and hindrances that could affect your progression in life.

Names	Hindrances

| What will you do to remove or change these hindrances?

Many times, we find ourselves displaying a loyalty that far exceeds others' expectations. We take our allegiance to heart, expecting to receive the same. However, many people never reciprocate what we put out. For some reason, we continue this loyalty until it costs us dearly. Sapphira did not seem to be dedicated to anything or anyone other than her husband. Misguided love can override our desire to do what's right.

| Describe what loyalty means to you. What will you sacrifice to maintain your loyalty?

We take loyalty to mean that we are to remain by someone's side no matter what he or she does. This is what Sapphira did for Ananias. It was literally unto death. She put her trust in man and not God. This is not what God wants for us. We must be committed to Him and no one else. God did not have a problem with Sapphira's loyalty. It was who she was loyal to that was the problem. She placed her loyalty in her dishonest husband. God doesn't want the Thelma-and-Louise type of allegiance; He wants the kind of loyalty Jesus demonstrated as He went to the cross. God is not pleased when we commit a wrongful act, then attempt to conceal it, and put it off as a form of loyalty. Upholding lies for our benefit exposes our true sinful nature. Sapphira was the original OG, the ride-or-die chick, and look where she ended up. As a lesson to all of us, God wants loyalty, but He wants an honest, unadulterated commitment to Him. There is no one more loyal than God. In Deuteronomy 31:6 and Hebrews 13:5, God said He would never leave us or forsake us. When we are unfaithful, He is still faithful. However, God does not uphold wrongdoings. He will not go along with our lies and deceit. We must do as God would do and not allow our loyalty to destroy our character.

> Have you ever allowed your loyalty to supersede your decision to do what's right? If so, what was the outcome? If not, how did you stay on the right path?

My Testimony

There was a time in my life when loyalty was all I focused on. The type of men I was attracted to in my earlier years called for loyalty that no one would ever understand. I did some unthinkable things that should have landed me in jail. I would lie just to save face with the man I thought I was madly in love with. I always prided myself on being strong, independent, and a force to be reckoned with, but there were times when I was not sure who I was. I pretended to be one person externally, but internally, I was someone different. Lies, loyalty, and death were becoming the norm for me. I lied about everything. It had gotten so bad that I could not tell the difference between the truth and a lie.

My loyalty nearly cost me my freedom. The death I faced was that of my soul. There was so much betrayal within me until I felt nothing. I felt dead on the inside due to all the corruption that consumed my heart and mind. Just like Sapphira, I chose that path of infidelity and enjoyed every moment. I knew what I was supporting was not right, but I did not care. All I wanted was the man I was upholding and the life I was living. Nothing else mattered to me at that time. I was consumed by infatuation, lust, money, and everything you could imagine. The only thing I was not concerned with was my life. You see, I was playing a dangerous game. I was living life in a backslidden state, which was not a good position to be in. I knew at any given moment I could forfeit my life. But, unlike Sapphira, God had mercy on me and spared my life. I learned in all of this that some of us would get another chance, whereas others may only have one chance. The scary part is, that we don't know whom God will grant a furlough for and whom He will call on home. This is why we should always live for Him. We should make decisions based on what He has instructed us to do. This way, we know that as long as we live for Jesus and not man, we have a better chance of surviving the worst of times and not making some life-costing decisions.

Prayer

Father God, I come boldly before You, giving You honor, praise, and glory. Lord, I know You've called me to be loyal in every way, but I need You to guide me because I can be devoted to a fault. My loyalty should not cause me to sin against You. On the contrary, it should strengthen our relationship. I want the type of loyalty Jesus has. He is loyal to You, God. He is faithful to us. He never does anything outside of Your commands. Help me to be like Christ, oh God. Reveal to me the true person when I'm making decisions to be there for someone. I need to discern who is for me and who is against me so I will not fall prey to their evil tricks and deeds. I don't want to get caught up in their world, Father. Give me the strength to resist lying, cheating, and committing all acts You disapprove of. Thank You for discernment, Your faithfulness, wisdom to make the right decisions, and the strength to resist the temptation that continually besets me. It is in Your Son, Jesus's name I pray, amen!

Notes

Chapter Four
GOD'S PLAN WILL ALWAYS PREVAIL

Jehosheba (Ja hosh uba)
2 KINGS 11:2-3 (NASB)

²But Jehosheba, the daughter of King Joram (jo'-ram), sister of Ahaziah, (ey-uh-zahy-uh) took Joash the son of Ahaziah and stole him from among the king's sons who were being put to death, and placed him and his nurse in the bedroom. So they hid him from Athaliah (ath-uh-lahy-uh), and he was not put to death. ³So he was hidden with her in the house of the Lord six years, while Athaliah was reigning over the land.

Her Story

Jehosheba, daughter of King Jehoram of Judah, sister to King Ahaziah of Judah, and wife of Jehoiada, the priest, was a brave woman.

Being the daughter of a king and wife of a priest, she knew the ramifications of disobeying a direct order from the self-proclaimed queen, Athaliah, had she been caught. Can you imagine what she may have been feeling as she blatantly violated orders of the land? Even though she could have been put to death for her disobedience, she still dared to step up and save the future king of Judah, Joash. All the other sons were murdered. She took him and hid him in the temple, in the safety of God's presence, for six years. Upon the seventh year, he was brought forth to take his rightful place on the throne. The number seven represents something being finished or completed. Jehosheba played an integral part in God's plan. He used someone in an important position to carry out His ultimate plan. Daughter and sister of kings, wife of a prominent priest, and stepdaughter of a queen is no small position. We know it was because God chose her for this daunting, risky task that she could accomplish such a paramount assignment.

Joash reigned for forty years in Jerusalem because God used Jehosheba to save him from the wrath of Athaliah when he was a baby. There are several people God is saving for specific times in our society. When that time comes, He will reveal those He has called to complete His tasks.

Describe a time where you disobeyed instructions for the good of your future.

She was kindhearted, selfless, compassionate, and unyielding in her quest to save Joash. Her success in protecting the future king depended on her ability to remain in hiding until it was time for Joash to be announced as king. She used her good qualities to save the future king. The love she had for her country and her nephew superseded any consequences she could have faced if she had been caught.

Which of the above characteristics/acts can you identify with? Explain.

In the table below, list the traits you possess that God can use. Then, describe how you can use them to help someone you love.

Traits You Possess	Usefulness

Protecting Joash by hiding him had to be an act of God. How could someone steal a child right from under the servants? It was truly a miracle to have taken him and his nurse and placed them in another room without being seen. God shielded them from death to fulfill His purpose in both their lives. He did not allow Jehosheba to be seen by anyone who could have destroyed them. This is what God does. He shields us from danger while we are right in the midst of it. Imagine having a life-threatening experience, and just as you thought the end was inevitable, God comes in, swoops you up out of danger, and shields you by hiding you from all that could destroy you. When He has a plan for you, He will not allow any harm to come upon you. He will always protect you, but you must be obedient to His plan.

> Describe a time when God shielded you and allowed you to break free from a possibly disastrous situation. How did you feel after it was all over?

Application

Jehosheba took her nephew, Joash, to the temple. The temple is the holy place of God. It is where His presence resides. She and Joash remained there for six years without detection. God will place a covering over you amid danger and turmoil if you're obedient. Being and staying in God's presence is predicated on your obedience.

> Describe how you feel when you are in God's presence.

In the seventh year, Joash came out of hiding and took his rightful place. During the six years, Jehosheba played a part in Joash's growth and maturity.

When God has us in hiding, many great things will happen.

1. We are strengthened.
2. We gain a tremendous amount of endurance.
3. We learn how to be patient.
4. We understand what it means to wait on God and not get in a hurry.
5. Knowledge and wisdom are imparted to us.
6. We should no longer be fearful of what may happen because God is the one who is hiding us.
7. We learn how to prepare for what's to come strategically.

There's a great deal happening when we are hiding in the presence of the Lord. We are not idle. We are diligently working on walking in our destiny.

Write some steps you need to take to gain access to God's presence. Then, check (✓) done as you accomplish it.

	Steps Needed	Done
1.		
2.		
3.		
4.		
5.		
6.		
7.		
8.		
9.		
10.		

My Testimony

Finding myself lost in a world that offered nothing but chaos, destruction, and heartache, I was speedily approaching a never-ending cycle of what appeared to be a life of safety presented by the enemy himself. It nearly cost me everything. I was on a downward spiral toward a life of regret.

I can relate to Jehosheba because my grandmother was the one who hid me via her prayers as I treaded blindly through life. She asked God to cover and protect me from the hands of the enemy who was so desperately trying to destroy me by using deceitful tactics. Unfortunately, what he placed right before my eyes was enticing, and I fell prey to much of it. I took advantage of men, wrote hot checks, dated drug dealers because of all the material things they could purchase for me, and so much more. These are just a few tactics the enemy would use to entice me.

I found myself slipping into a world that would land me in bondage forever. It was because she labored in prayer day and night for my safety that I was saved from the inevitable destruction.

During most of my childhood—and some of my teenage years—I was forced to attend shut-in services, also known as revivals. I now know this was my grandmother's way of making sure the enemy could not completely dismantle my life. She hid me in the house of the Lord at every opportunity she had while I was young so that when I grew older, God's word and spirit would always be with me.

One day I came to my senses and realized the error of my ways. The enemy could no longer destroy me. Now, I am forever covered in the blood of Jesus.

Father God, hiding in Your presence is the only way I can ensure I'll remain safe at all times. Help me to holdfast right where You have me. I know that when You are ready for me to surface, You will let me know. It is not easy avoiding the enemy's tricks. This is why I depend on You to keep me safe. Keep my mind and ways in line with Your ways. Don't take Your hands off me. I'm thankful that I can rest assured, You'll always be with me. You said You'd never leave me nor forsake me, and knowing that You are a God of Your word, I can rest peacefully. I don't have to worry or try and figure out my next step because You've already taken care of that. Thank You for hiding me from the hands of the enemy and keeping me safe until my appointed time. Thank You for choosing me to do great works on behalf of You, oh Lord. Thank You for imprinting upon my heart the love You have for me. With that, I know I can depend on You for *everything*. Thank You for just being Lord over my life. It is in Your Son, Jesus's name, I pray, amen!

Notes

Chapter Five
OBEDIENCE PAYS OFF

Shiphrah (Shif' ruh) and Puah (Pū´a)
EXODUS 1:15–21 (HCSB)

¹⁵Then the king of Egypt said to the Hebrew midwives, one of whom was named Shiphrah and the other Puah, ¹⁶"When you help the Hebrew women give birth, observe them as they deliver, If the child is a son, kill him, but if it is a daughter, she may live." ¹⁷The Hebrew midwives, however, feared God and did not do as the king of Egypt had told them; they let the boys live. ¹⁸So the king of Egypt summoned the midwives and asked them, "Why have you done this and let the boys live?" ¹⁹The midwives said to Pharaoh, "The Hebrew women are not like the Egyptian women, for they are vigorous and give birth before a midwife can get to them." ²⁰So God was good to the midwives, and the people multiplied and became very numerous. ²¹Since the midwives feared God, He gave them families.

Their Story

Shiphrah and Puah were Hebrew midwives serving under the leadership of the pharaoh. They cared for the Hebrew women during childbirth. They did not have families of their own; however, they did not show any bitterness or envy toward God. They also didn't blame Him for their barrenness. Instead, they freely gave of their time, hearts, and gifts to assist the needs of others.

Two extraordinary women showed bravery, faith, and fear of God through their disobedience to the pharaoh. Shiphrah and Puah could have been killed for disobeying the pharaoh. Instead, their fear of God led them to carry out a task pleasing in His sight, as opposed to delivering unto the king of Egypt what he commanded, and that was the death of all the sons of the Hebrew women. There were many midwives during this time. Shiphrah and Puah's desire to please God and not man played a significant role in God's overall plan to protect His people. These women were willing to risk their lives for God.

After the pharaoh found out they were defying his order, he called them in for a meeting. He wanted to know their motives for allowing the baby boys to live. They informed the king of the rapid birth of the Hebrew women, insinuating that there would never be enough time to reach them before delivery. Pharaoh believed them because he did not have them put to death.

Due to their fear of God, along with their unselfish, sacrificing hearts, God blessed them with their own families. It pleased God to see that Shiphrah and Puah revered Him so much that no man could get them to go against God. Due to their determination to ensure God was pleased and honored, the Hebrews multiplied tremendously throughout Egypt.

> To please God, sometimes you must go against others. How far are you willing to go to please God? What will you lose or gain?

Your desire to please God should override any request received from other people. We should follow God's commands and instructions at all costs. Shiphrah and Puah knew what they were up against, but they chose to disobey the pharaoh and obey God, despite the possible consequences they could face.

> Describe a time when you had to choose between God and others (family members and friends). Describe the impact your decision had on the relationship (positive or negative).

Have you ever disobeyed God and decided to follow other people instead? Describe what happened?

List the emotions you felt as you decided to obey or disobey God.

OBEYED GOD	DISOBEYED GOD

This had to be a difficult decision for Shiphrah and Puah. Knowing they could be put to death for defying the king's order had to be terrifying. Yet they chose God over man. Their relationship with the Almighty God superseded their human duty to obey the king. God blessed their obedience. Receiving their reward from God had to be a highlight of their lives. God gave them the ultimate gift—families of their own.

| Discuss a tough decision you've had to make. What did it cost you?

In life, you will have difficult decisions to make. You can choose to obey or disobey the commands of God. Just know: if you go against God, the consequences will be a daunting experience that you are not ready for. But if you obey Him, the reward and blessing will be an exhilarating encounter.

| Do you find it hard to obey God's commands? Why or why not?

Application

God used two midwives to save Israel's children as part of His ultimate plan. The very women who served the pharaoh were faithful servants of God in their hearts. Because of their heart-to-heart relationship, they wanted nothing more than to please their Lord. Their intentional disobedience to the pharaoh showed this. Although they could have lost their lives, they did not allow that to interfere with their decision. Thwarting the pharaoh's plan was more important than defying the God they served and loved.

You may be asked to do or say something that goes against everything you believe in. It could cost you your job or a relationship you hold dear to your heart. You may be asked to go somewhere that you know is not an appropriate place to be. What will you do?

| How would you handle putting God's plan before your own?

| Describe the strength of your relationship with Christ.

List some areas in your life that you believe would be hard to let go.

_____
_____
_____
_____
_____
_____
_____
_____

List the strengths you see in Shiphrah and Puah and your strengths.

Shiphrah and Puah's Strengths	Your Strengths

Are there any similarities in your strengths? How can you use your strengths to glorify God?

After reading the story of the midwives, did you find any weaknesses in them? If so, what were they? Now, list them and discuss the similarities.

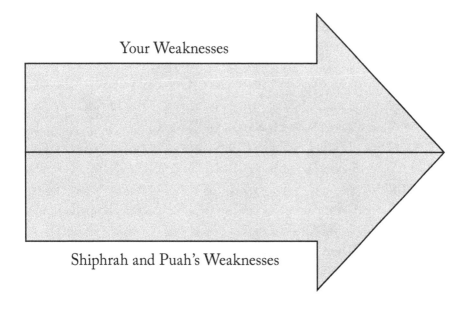

Your Weaknesses

Shiphrah and Puah's Weaknesses

My Testimony

Having to choose between God and my desires was not easy at first. Although I was raised in the church, it still was challenging for me to decide which I wanted most: God or the world. On the other hand, it felt good to do the things I was doing, show up at the places I chose to explore, and say whatever came to mind without hesitation or caring how it impacted others. That was my life, and I loved it. I always knew in my heart that I should be following Jesus, but because of my quest to do my own thing, I rebelled and paid dearly.

I was not like Shiphrah and Puah, more committed to God than to others. They took a chance based on their faith. I did the opposite. I took a chance based on my own free will. The world was fun, promising, adventurous, and enticing. Following Christ did not seem to offer what the world offered.

After a while, things seemed repetitive. I was continually doing the same things: drinking, partying, and you can imagine all the other ungodly acts I committed. I was fighting a losing battle, and the only way to win was to follow Jesus. One day I was finally tired of being disobedient. It was at this moment that I decided to give Jesus a try. I was ready to go all out for Christ.

As I read the story of these two women, I wondered why I chose the route of disobedience instead of being obedient and traveling the path God set before me. Until this day, I can only attribute my disobedience to wanting to fulfill my fleshly desires. I knew I should have been following God from the beginning. Nothing should have deterred me. When I realized that living for Jesus was much better than dabbling in the world, I gave my heart to Him, and I haven't looked back.

I now know that choosing Jesus was the right choice.

Father God, thank You for giving me a chance to get back on the right path. Thank You for never leaving me to myself. Thank You for patiently waiting on me to choose You. Lord, You did not allow me to remain in the state I was in, and for that, I'm grateful. Even though I was headed for destruction, You kept me covered in Your grace and mercy. You did not allow any permanent harm to come to me, and for that, I'm grateful. Lord, learning to follow You instead of other people was a hard lesson for me to grasp, but now, looking back, it was not as hard as I made it. Thank You for sending reminders to me, letting me know that I belong to You. I ignored many of them in the beginning, but eventually, I started listening and obeying. Thank You, oh Lord, for Your faithfulness to me. I don't deserve all that You've given me, but I do appreciate it. Thank You for just being Lord over my life. I love You, Lord, with all my heart. It is in Your Son, Jesus's name, I pray, amen!

Notes

Chapter Six
SEEKING JUSTICE, GIVE US WHAT WE DESERVE

The Daughters of Zelophehad
Mahla (MAH-luh:), Noah (NOE-uh:),
Hoglah (HOG-luh), Milcah (MILL-kuh),
Tirzah (TUR-zuh)

NUMBERS 27:1–7 (NASB)

¹Then the daughters of Zelophehad, the son of Hepher, the son of Gilead, the son of Machir, the son of Manasseh, of the families of Manasseh the son of Joseph, came near; and these are the names of his daughters: Mahlah, Noah and Hoglah and Milcah and Tirzah. ² And they stood before Moses and before Eleazar the priest and before the leaders and all the congregation, at the doorway of the tent of meeting, saying, ³"Our father died in the wilderness, yet he was not among the company of those who gathered themselves together against the Lord in the company of Korah; but he died in his own sin, and he had no sons. ⁴ "Why should the name of our father be withdrawn from among his family because he had no son? Give us a possession among our father's brothers. ⁵And Moses brought their case before the Lord. ⁶Then the Lord spoke to Moses, saying, ⁷"The daughters of Zelophehad are right in their statements. You shall surely give them a hereditary possession among their father's brothers, and you shall transfer the inheritance of their father to them."

Their Story

The daughters of Zelophehad stood together to claim their inheritance. They were not rude or disrespectful, but they were firm in their stance for what they believed was rightly theirs. They logically presented their case.

During this time, daughters had no rights. The sons received all inheritance from the fathers. However, Zelophehad did not have any sons. So his estate was not given to anyone, and his clan would've been wiped out due to his untimely death. Zelophehad's daughters weren't going to allow that to happen, so they petitioned Moses, Eleazar (the priest), the leaders, and the entire community regarding their right to their father's inheritance.

They knew that if they did not stand up, their inheritance would be gone forever. So their stance was critical for many reasons. One reason was that they made it known that their father was not part of the rebellion. Therefore, punishing them by keeping their inheritance was unjust.

It took great intelligence, courage, discipline, and planning for these ladies to go before the authorities and petition for their inheritance. They had to maintain their composure as they sought justice in a manner that was pleasing in God's sight. Fighting for something they knew they deserved had to make them nervous, which could have brought about a different outcome.

Let's explore a different scenario. Mahla, Noah, Hoglah, Milcah, and Tirzah realized all the other clans were receiving an inheritance. They were the only ones who were not a part of the process. They came together and decided to approach Moses. When they approached him, they could've been unprepared to present their case. Each one could've had a different perspective of what and how they should receive their inheritance. They did not have to be of one accord, which would've disrupted their intent to present their case, thereby leaving Moses to think they weren't capable of receiving and keeping such an inheritance. Remember, by law, only the sons were supposed to obtain inheritance. Moses did not have to listen to them. But because of their togetherness, preparedness, unwavering approach, and respect for him and his position, he listened. These women knew they were going up against the law of God, and they had to present their case in a manner that would get the attention needed.

Seeking justice can be a daunting task in the process of receiving what's rightfully yours. However, because the sisters' hearts and motives were pure, God instructed Moses to give them their inheritance. Their persistence and ability to stand together and not quarrel with the leaders brought about a victory for them. They received what they deserved, and because of their petition, God made a change in the inheritance laws. When things are done decently and in order, God will always reward us.

What have you petitioned God for that you feel is rightfully yours? How did you approach the situation?

Many characteristics were displayed through Mahla, Noah, Hoglah, Milcah, and Tirzah. They did not approach the situation with a militant mindset. However, they did not allow themselves to be overlooked because of their gender.

Intelligence, courage, discipline, respect, persistence, boldness, and patience were attributes displayed as they petitioned Moses and the leaders over the camp.

It takes a great deal of intelligence to know the laws and present your case in a manner worthy of examination. Had they not been intelligent, the plan to approach Moses and the leaders would not have prevailed as it did. They were victorious because they stood together with a solid plan.

Circle the attributes that you see in yourself. If there are other attributes you have, negative or positive, that are not listed, write them around the cross.

Intelligent

Humble   Deceitful

Disciplined   Vengeful   Merciful

Prideful   Bold   Compassionate   Patient

Respectful   Persistent   Courageous

Arrogant   Unforgiving

Jubilant   Spiteful

Just like Mahla, Noah, Hoglah, Milcah, and Tirzah, we all have great qualities. However, depending on circumstances, many of us demonstrate more of our negative attributes than positive ones. Therefore, we must learn to approach our situations from a positive perspective, no matter how undesirable they may be. Unfortunately, this is difficult to do because our flesh immediately steps in and wants to take control.

They appropriately fought for justice. They were calm and presented their case with tact and intellect. They were not rowdy, disruptive, loud, or disrespectful. Unfortunately, some of us allow our fight to become a fleshly fight instead of a spiritual one. Learning how to obtain what we are seeking, we must first learn to control our approach.

> Discuss the attributes you circled. Then, explain why you chose those.

At some point in our lives, all of us will have to deal with the negativity that haunts us. We must learn to approach every situation we face with a positive outlook, and the only way we can successfully do this is by consulting God. Having the proper perspective, attitude, knowledge, and patience will always set us ahead eventually.

> Why is it easier to lean toward negative emotions and feelings when we fight for something we believe we have a right to? Explain.

Application

There are many different ways to handle any situation you may face. However, your attitude and demeanor play a big part in whether you'll be successful or not. We often want the results to be in our favor, but we will lose without the proper approach.

How you present your case is critical. Instead of bearing a defiant tone when you state your case, try being humble and polite. Frequently, you will allow your determination to get something resolved and push you toward the "Oh, they're going to listen to me or else" attitude. But in reality, you want something from them—not the other way around. Therefore, toning down your behavior would benefit you more in the end.

We fight for many things in our lives. But whether it is fighting for our jobs or keeping our families together, we understand that it takes strategic planning to win.

> For those who have taken the more undesirable approach, how did that work out for you? If you haven't done any of these, have you seen it done?

| Why do you think women tend to be more thunderous than men?

| Describe how you would've handled the same situation as the five daughters. Explain your answer.

Take a deep look within and examine your inner person. What do you see?

Are you a mirror image of the daughters? If so, explain. If not, do you possess the opposite characteristics? Explain.

Write the words in the circle that you are feeling at this moment. Reflect upon them for a moment and then pray that God will increase the positive emotions and remove the negative ones. Name them as you are praying.

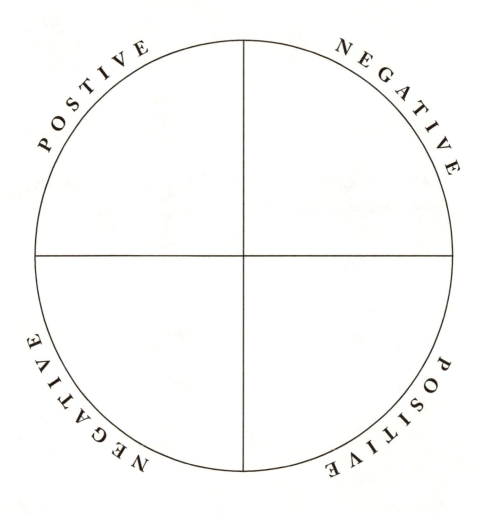

Discuss your positive traits. How can those traits help you be successful?

My Testimony

I've been in a situation where I had to fight for a position I felt I deserved. I was overlooked, and it was not fair. After approaching my boss and presenting my case professionally, just as the five daughters had, he listened and called a meeting with his direct reports.

A week had passed, and I had not heard a word. Finally, a week and a half later, he called me into his office and stated that they needed someone with a little more experience. I was devastated because I had been there for five years, and when the position became available, I filled in temporarily while fulfilling my other duties. This was not fair at all. They hired an older lady, who they claimed had more experience than I did. However, that was not the case. She knew absolutely nothing about the job she was hired to do. They asked me to train her. I politely and happily declined. I told them it was my understanding they were hiring an experienced person. Since I was not qualified to fill the position, I am not qualified to train anyone.

Was that the proper way to handle this situation? Probably not, but I was in my early twenties and did not have nearly as much tact and respect as I have now. I tried the respectful approach, and it got me nowhere. I was not successful in my quest to be promoted. However, it felt good telling them no. They did not like my response. Soon after that, the environment became a miserable place to work. I ended up quitting.

Fast-forward to thirty years later. If I were presented with the same challenge, I would do it differently. I would pray first. (I did not do that back then.) Then, after getting the go-ahead from God, I would pursue what I felt was rightfully mine. On the other hand, if God instructed me to stand still, I would do just that. I have learned that seeking God first in all that I do is the best *first* step to take. After that, He always guided me in the direction I should go. The daughters of Zelophehad had Moses. Going to him in the manner they did allowed their case to be presented before God, and they won. Unfortunately, because I followed my heart and not my intellect and charisma, I lost.

Prayer

Father God, thank You for my intelligence and ability to approach situations in a manner pleasing to You. Thank You for setting guidelines so that I have no reason to lose focus. Without Your guidance, I would be in a whirlwind of trouble because my way of doing things is far from Yours. I have learned how to seek You first before approaching any situation. I know that You will go ahead of me and make my crooked path straight. You will touch the hearts of those who need it so that I will be successful. You will open doors that should be opened and close those that should be closed. I have to be patient and wait on You to move on my behalf. Give me the confidence and assurance I need when facing a situation that will require someone to grant me what I'm seeking. Lord, I thank You for always being here for me. Thank You for leading me in a direction that will catapult me into the next phase of my life. Thank You for giving me all that You have promised. It is in Your Son, Jesus's name, I pray, amen!

Notes

Chapter Seven
WEARING WISDOM WELL

Abigail
1 SAMUEL 25:24-25; 27-28; 32-35 (HCSB)

²⁴She fell at his feet and said, "The guilt is mine, my lord, but please let your servant speak to you directly. Listen to the words of your servant. ²⁵My lord should pay no attention to this worthless man Nabal, for he lives up to his name: His name is Nabal, and stupidity is all he knows. I, your servant, did not see my lord's young men whom you sent. ²⁷Accept this gift your servant has brought to my lord, and let it be given to the young men who follow my lord. ²⁸Please forgive your servant's offense, for the Lord is certain to make a lasting dynasty for my lord because he fights the Lord's battles. Throughout your life, may evil not be found in you. ³²Then David said to Abigail, "Praise to the Lord God of Israel, who sent you to meet me today! ³³Your discernment is blessed, and you are blessed. Today you kept me from participating in bloodshed and avenging myself by my own hand. ³⁴Otherwise, as surely as the Lord God of Israel lives, who prevented me from harming you, if you had not come quickly to meet me, Nabal wouldn't have had any men left by morning light. ³⁵then David accepted what she had brought him and said, "Go home in peace. See, I have heard what you said and have granted your request."

Her Story

Abigail was married to a wealthy rancher named Nabal. She was intelligent and beautiful. However, her husband was harsh and evil in all his dealings. We have heard that opposites attract! Well, here's the perfect example of a man and woman with different personalities, goals, and agendas attracted to one another.

> Explain how it feels to be attracted to someone different from you.

Nabal was a fool and would not listen to reason. On the other hand, Abigail was wise and intentional about every move she made. Her wisdom was evident in how she handled the news she received from one of Nabal's young men.

> Dealing with a foolish person cannot be easy. If this were you, explain how you would have handled him (your spouse, fiancé, boyfriend, etc.)

After hearing about David's request and her husband's response, she immediately jumped into action to save her family. First, she used her intellect, wisdom, and charm to win David's respect, and later, after the death of her husband, she won his love.

She humbly submitted to him as she pleaded her case. But, along with that submission, she brought gifts for both him and his men. She knew David was going to attack and kill them. But she was quick on her feet, and her swiftness to act saved their lives.

David was impressed with her ability to calm him and reconsider attacking Nabal's family. She won the heart of David by speaking the truth and showing how politically astute she was. Without Abigail's astuteness, charisma, and quick thinking, the outcome would have been devastating.

> Which of your personality traits would have surfaced if you faced a situation like Abigail?

David received her kind speech well. She was very discreet in her approach. When dealing with someone who had great power, she knew she had to be very diplomatic and straightforward. Abigail knew that if she petitioned David on his premises, she had a better chance at winning him over. This showed her brilliance and knack for recognizing who she was petitioning.

> Have you or someone you know ever had a situation occur where you had to approach someone in power? Explain your approach.

Many of us have or will have to stand up for ourselves and our families. But, just like Abigail, we need to be wise in our approach in dealing with a situation that could turn fatal. We want to be heard, but to do this, we must use wisdom.

David recognized Abigail's wisdom from the very beginning because of the way she entered his presence. She was in a lethal crisis, but she did not let that impede her ability to appeal to him honorably. She did not allow her circumstance to change her character. All it did was uncover who she truly was, a wise woman.

> Think about a situation you encountered unexpectedly. Did you allow it to take you out of character? How did you handle it?

Using wisdom will always give you the upper hand over those who do not use wisdom. So, there is no reason why any of us should walk around foolishly using lousy judgment. If we ask God for wisdom, He will give it to us (James 1:5-8). He gave it to Abigail, and since He is the same today, yesterday, and forever, He'll do the same for us.

List some situations that required wisdom. Discuss whether or not you used it. Discuss the outcome. Think about how things could have turned out had you used wisdom. Describe the outcome.

Situation/Problem	Used Wisdom	Did Not Use Wisdom	Outcome

Abigail had to smother the spark before it turned into an uncontrollable flame. Her husband had no idea she was interceding for her family. First, she had to formulate a plan, then proceed without his knowledge. Had Abigail informed him of her strategy to plead her case before David, he would have intervened and prohibited her from moving forward.

> Think of a time you had to take care of an issue without the knowledge of your spouse or someone dear to you. What were the actions necessary for you to handle the pressing issue at hand?

Abigail's interpersonal skills were awe-inspiring. Any time a woman can change a man's mind who is angry and ready to kill, she has a gift to extinguish confrontation successfully. Some of us ignite the fires, whereas others, just like Abigail, will dowse it.

> When a damaging situation flares up in your life, what's your initial reaction? Are you quick to extinguish or ignite? Explain.

Application

All of us confront our enemies differently. Sometimes we lash out in anger without realizing what we've done. We don't think about the consequences before we react. All we think about is handling them before they get the best of us. We don't use wisdom, nor do we consult God first.

> How do you respond to your enemies? Are you impulsive or strategic in your quest to resolve whatever problems you may have with others? Explain.

However, some of us are wise in our approach to dealing with our enemies. Before reacting, we think about and visualize the entire scene before speaking a word or physically moving forward. We consider the outcome beforehand, which gives us the upper hand. Confrontation should reveal the wisdom in us, not the foolishness.

Which do you exhibit in a life-threatening situation, wisdom or foolishness? Explain your answer.

It takes a tremendous amount of strength to refrain from acting on impulse. However, when we can show others that we can handle a life-threatening situation, we reveal our character of unshakable wisdom, knowledge, and power without making it worse.

The man who worked for Abigail's husband knew she was a notably wise and strong woman. This is why he brought the problem to her. He knew she would handle it with a precise and calculated strategy.

What will others say about your ability to handle chaos in your life? Do wisdom, knowledge, and power show, or is it the opposite?

Write your problem(s) below and how you would solve them on the sides.

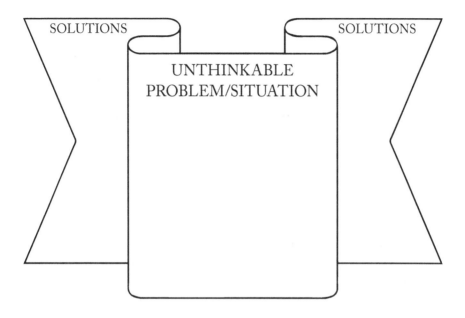

My Testimony

Dating a drug dealer in my early twenties was not the smartest thing I did, but it happened. I can relate to facing a life-threatening situation because I found myself sitting right in the middle of the devil's den. I most remember being frightened while trying to show no fear and nervous while trying to remain calm. I not only placed my life in danger unknowingly, but I also placed my children's lives in danger as well. It took me a few years to realize that my actions were foolish and reckless. It was time for me to wise up. I knew the dealer had a temper, and if my demeanor was not right when I approached him, only God knew what could've happened.

Usually, a life such as this doesn't receive compassion or understanding. I was ready to get out, but I could not just leave. I knew too much. Remember, I have children. I prayed and asked God to get me out. I no longer wanted to date him and be a part of that life. I had been in it long enough. I'd seen so much that I realized this was not what I wanted for my girls or me when I came to my senses.

My wisdom and intellect kicked in, and I went back to what I knew: prayer. Eventually, God worked it out for me. Had I done what I wanted to do and left, only God knows what could've happened. The dealer was arrested one day on his way to take me to lunch. I visited him and told him I did not want to end up in jail or dead. I had two girls to raise, and this was no life for them. Miraculously, he agreed. I was released from that unproductive and dangerous life because I used wisdom and put it in God's hands. He changed the dealer's heart.

Prayer

Father God, thank You for reminding us that wisdom comes from You, and any time we find ourselves in a hopeless situation, all we have to do is call on You. You will tell us what to say and how to say it. You will guide our actions. You will remove the threat right before our eyes. You have blessed us with wisdom, knowledge, and understanding, but sometimes we forget and want to handle things our way. Help us be more like Abigail and approach all our problems with astuteness, charisma, and patience. Nothing good can come from us acting foolishly. Thank You for always being there for us. Thank You for not allowing our emotions to overrule the wisdom You've placed in us. Thank You for keeping us as we deal with whatever comes our way. It is in Your Son, Jesus's name I pray, amen!

Notes

Chapter Eight
A SELFLESS ACT

Achsah
JOSHUA 15:18-19 (HCSB)

¹⁸When she arrived, she persuaded Othniel to ask her father for a field. As she got off her donkey, Caleb asked her, "What do you want?" ¹⁹She replied, "Give me a blessing. Since you have given me land in the Negev, give me the springs of water also." So he gave her the upper and lower springs.

Her Story

Achsah was Caleb's daughter and wife to his nephew, Othniel. After being given away to Othniel, she persuaded him to ask her father, Caleb, to give them land because she had no legal right to obtain any inheritance. Only sons had that right. After Caleb gave them the land, he asked her directly what she wanted. She told him a blessing. She not only wanted the land in the Negev he had already given her, but she wanted the springs of water as well. Her father honored her request and blessed her with the upper and lower springs. Achsah received what she desired because she was not afraid to ask for what she wanted. Not only was she not scared, she knew exactly what she wanted. She did not hesitate, nor did she shy away from her desire to own land and the springs.

> What is it that you desire but hesitate to ask for? Why the hesitation?

Achsah knew the springs of water she asked for would make the land productive. But she looked to the future and saw they needed more than what she initially received for her and her husband to provide a prosperous future for their family.

> When you plan for your future, what is it that you need to have a better life? Explain.

She received all that she asked from her father. She did not exhibit greediness by asking for more than she truly needed. Because she asked for what was required, Caleb gave her more. He gave her both the upper and lower springs. He did not have to do this. He could've given her one of the springs.

> When you set your mind on something, how do you proceed? What's your attitude toward receiving what you desire?

We all have many wants. We plan, and some of us even plot to acquire all that we desire. As we pursue our wishes, we should be like Achsah: humble, selfless, bold, and respectful. We can get more with kindness and humility than we can with a lack thereof. We need to learn how to execute a plan without exhibiting a hostile, aggressive attitude. Achsah was confident and sure of what she wanted, and we must emulate her behavior. When asked the question, "What do you want?" we should be able to answer without hesitation. Know what you want and ask for it. She was not afraid to ask her father for more.

> What do you want? How do you plan to get it? Explain.

List your wants and your plan of action to get what you want.

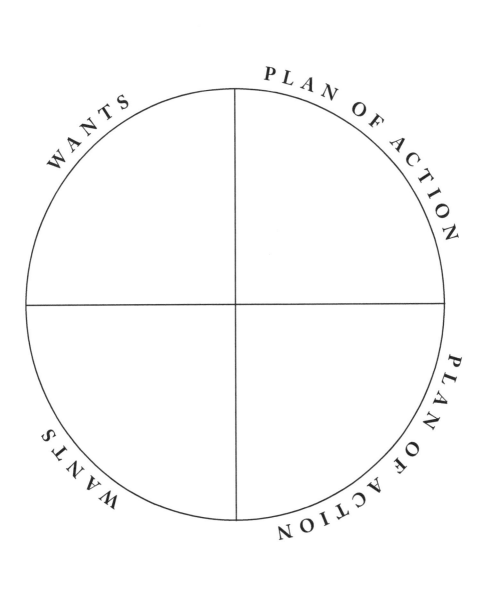

We can think of many reasons Achsah would want more land and springs of water. Knowing her character, we can presume it was to benefit her future family. However, she was not a selfish person. She was clever and calculating, but also humble and respectful.

> What are your reasons for wanting more? Explain.

Achsah placed herself in a position of readiness by knowing precisely what she wanted and how to get it. Take a look back over your life. Think about everything you have asked for or wanted.

List a few of the things you've asked for and received; then list the things you did not receive. Finally, explain why you think you did not receive what you asked for.

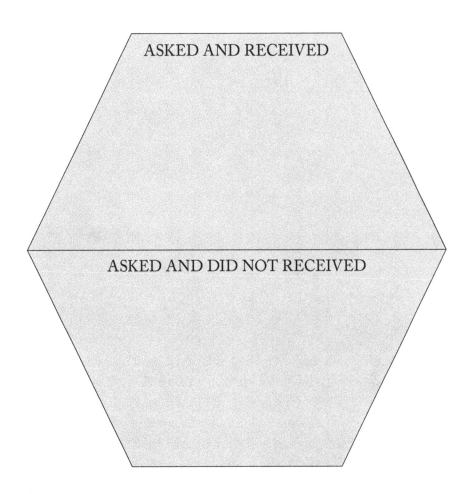

Application

To receive your heart's desire, you must put God first. For example, He could send someone to bless you or give you favor with others. Having a connection, understanding, or a special relationship with the person you're expecting a gift from could also help you obtain all that you desire.

> **What must you give up to receive what you're asking for? Explain.**

Achsah and Caleb had a special relationship, a father-daughter bond that no one could break. In the culture Achsah grew up in, women weren't allowed to receive an inheritance. But she boldly asked for the land and springs of water because of her relationship and influence. Had her relationship with her father been rocky, she probably wouldn't have felt comfortable requesting either. It takes a strong, confident woman to pursue what she genuinely wants in life. But, in that confidence, she must be wise. Without wisdom that comes from God and boldness, many will lose out on a great deal.

Who do you have a close relationship with? Can you ask them for anything and know they will give it to you?

Explain why you believe you would receive all that you ask from this person.

Having a good rapport with people is extremely important. It is that rapport that will open doors of opportunity for each of us. For example, Achsah not only had a good connection with her father, Caleb, but we know she must have had a close relationship with God. Knowing that only the sons were entitled to land and inheritance, God allowed her to be blessed by her father, who, by the way, had always been a faithful servant of God. Indeed, Caleb taught her to reverence God in all that she does. We must do the same. Ultimately, our blessings come from God. He uses people to give us everything we need—and some of what we want—here on earth. Therefore, we need to recognize who the real Giver is, and He is God.

Write the names of the people with whom you have a good rapport. If you went to them for anything, would they give it to you? Why or why not?

NAME OF PERSON	BESIDES THE RAPPORT, WHY WOULD THEY GIVE YOU WHAT YOU'VE ASKED FOR?

My Testimony

I had a great relationship with my father (not my biological father) as well. I was his baby girl, and I could get anything I wanted from him. All I had to do was ask. I learned at an early age that fathers tend to cater to their girls. So every time I needed anything, all I had to do was ask. I was not afraid, nor did I ever think I wouldn't receive what I wanted. Why? Because we had a father-daughter relationship that no one could break apart. Like Achsah, I was always respectful, humble, and used a great deal of wisdom when approaching my father. When it came to me, he had a heart of gold. But it was not just with me; he was that way with all of his girls. Being in his presence made me sure of who I was.

Because he loved me and wanted nothing but the best for me, I was able to excel beyond my expectations boldly. My relationship with him gave me the confidence I needed to succeed in life. Just as Achsah knew she'd be able to obtain all that she asked and it would help her in the future, I too recognized my father would give me the world, and his willingness to support me is what contributed to my success. What he instilled in me has stuck, and when I need it, I bring it to the surface. Being wise with the knowledge he'd given me was extremely important to my well-being.

Because of all that I would face later in life, I am glad my father and I had a close, loving relationship because that relationship helped me gain the strength I needed to survive. It taught me how not to be afraid to go after what I wanted. It showed me that having a rapport with people meant everything. Unfortunately, I did not execute any of this until much later in life. It was not until I matured that I truly understood what was planted deep inside me. I now know that it was all a part of God's plan for my father to be the man he was to me. I did not have a relationship with my biological father, so God gave me a replacement. He knew one day I would need a natural father. God always knows what we need and when we need it. I've learned not to discount relationships and rapport with others. One day, we'll need both to get us through some challenging times.

Prayer

Father God, thank You for being my spiritual Father. Thank You for being all-knowing and sending me the natural Father You knew I would need. Some women are not as fortunate as I was, and they grew up without a father. Teach us how to build lasting relationships. Help us establish a rapport with others. Give us courage and wisdom to ask for what we want, believing we will receive it. Keep us focused on what's suitable for our families and ourselves so that our motives are always pure. Thank You, Lord, for always being here for us. It is in Your Son, Jesus's name, I pray, amen!

Notes

Chapter Nine
A LUSTFUL HEART

Potiphar's Wife
GENESIS 39:6–18 (NASB)

⁶Now Joseph was handsome in form and appearance. ⁷It came about after these events that his master's wife looked with desire at Joseph, and she said, "Lie with me." ⁸But he refused and said to his master's wife, "Behold, with me *here*, my master does not concern himself with anything in the house, and he has put all that he owns in my charge.

⁹"There is no one greater in this house than I, and he has withheld nothing from me except you, because you are his wife. How then could I do this great evil and sin against God?" ¹⁰As she spoke to Joseph day after day, he did not listen to her to lie beside her *or* be with her. ¹¹Now it happened one day that he went into the house to do his work, and none of the men of the household was there inside.

¹²She caught him by his garment, saying, "Lie with me!" And he left his garment in her hand and fled, and went outside. ¹³When she saw that he had left his garment in her hand and had fled outside, ¹⁴she called to the men of her household and said to them, "See, he has brought in a Hebrew to us to make sport of us; he came in to me to lie with me, and I screamed. ¹⁵"When he heard that I raised my voice and screamed, he left his garment beside me and fled and went outside."

¹⁶So she left his garment beside her until his master came home. ¹⁷Then she spoke to him with these words, "The Hebrew slave, whom you brought to us, came in to me to make sport of me; ¹⁸and as I raised my voice and screamed, he left his garment beside me and fled outside."

Her Story

Potiphar's wife was relentless in going after someone who did not belong to her. She was in pursuit of having someone other than her husband. Not only was she in search of another man, but she was after God's man. She was blunt and did not care how Joseph perceived her. But, on the other hand, she was sneaky, conniving, mischievous, and a liar. All of these characteristics paint a picture of a dangerous woman to be around. She is the type of woman who will get you caught up in something you cannot get out of if you are not careful.

> Was there ever a time you pursued something or someone you knew was off-limits? If so, why did you continue with the pursuit? Explain.

Because of his love for God, faithfulness, and commitment to his master, he rejected her. He not only refused to entertain her once, but many times as she continued to try and persuade him to lie with her. She saw a good-looking man who had it all together, and she wanted to indulge in a sexual relationship with him. Potiphar's wife wanted her cake and ice cream too. She had a husband, but it seems he was not enough for her.

Potiphar's wife was the type of woman who would cause a man to lose everything. She had a plan, and regardless of the outcome, she was going to see to it that she would prevail sooner or later. She was persistent and would not take no for an answer. She wanted what she wanted, and if she could not have it, someone was going to pay.

When Joseph fled from her and left his garment in her hand, that was the perfect opportunity for her to repay him for his rejection. Or it could've been that, since the garment was there, what would she tell her husband when he saw it? She had to think and act fast. So she accused Joseph of trying to rape her, and it cost him his freedom. Women like Potiphar's wife exist all around us. They pursue men or things that are off-limits to them without hesitation. Their desires overtake their hormones and emotions and cause significant pain in many households. Potiphar's wife is the type of woman who will unmistakably cause great suffering in your relationships.

> What would it take to keep a woman such as this from causing conflict in your relationship?

Women are emotional beings who have desires that are sometimes beyond their control. Therefore, they seek after men who can fulfill those desires, even if the men are married or in a relationship. These women must know and understand that God will satisfy their hearts' desires if they turn to him and don't give in to their fleshly cravings. The enemy wants to use these distractions to destroy homes. However, the ones he is attempting to trick can defeat him by asking Jesus Christ to help them.

Some women are fighting to keep a happy marriage or relationship. Jesus has to be the foundation of their relationships for both the man and woman to overcome disruptions and distractions. If your husband or boyfriend loves Jesus Christ and refuses to go against His word, you'll have a good chance of avoiding such devastation in your relationships.

> Are you able to recognize the signs that your man is being pursued? If so, how? If not, explain.

List the signs that are easily recognizable in a man who a relentless woman is pursuing.

Take the signs listed above and begin to pray about them. Release those signs to God and then allow Him to contend with all that you have listed.

Now is not the time to give up and give in on your quest to stop this woman from destroying what God has brought together if you're married. If you are dating, and this will be your husband one day, the man God has for you, then you must be just as persistent in making sure that the work of God prevails in your relationship by praying, reading your Bible, and seeking after God together. There may be times when you will need advice or counseling from your pastor or someone who is serving Jesus. Surviving a Potiphar's wife is an enormous task, but it isn't impossible.

> What would you tell someone experiencing a Potiphar's wife situation? Explain.

Potiphar's wife did not care about the well-being of Joseph. All she cared about was satisfying herself. Nothing good ever comes from someone like this. Unfortunately, some of us have family and friends who resemble Potiphar's wife.

> Have you ever had a situation where you knew what your friend or a family member was doing was wrong, but you never said a word?

> If you tried to stop her or talk her out of what she was doing, did she listen? If not, what steps did you take next?

True friends will take heed to what you are saying. It is hard to infiltrate the hearts and minds of people who are on a mission to fulfill their desires, but it is up to us to be just as persistent as they are to help them overcome. You should never give up on your friends who mimic the characteristics of Potiphar's wife, and if you are the one with these flaws, you should seek after God and ask Him to deliver you. None of us are perfect. We are all struggling with something. This is why turning to God is the answer because He can mend a broken relationship and deliver the disrupter from her ways. He is no respecter of persons. The woman who emulates Potiphar's wife should want more and not want to settle for what someone else has. She must rid herself of all that is not Christlike and pursue Jesus to have what she is searching for.

Application

Some of us can relate to Potiphar's wife, whereas others cannot. We all share character flaws. They may not be the same ones Potiphar's wife had, but they are there. Even if we cannot see them, others can.

> If you can relate to her, identify the character flaw(s) that resembles you? Explain your answer.

> For those who have a different set of flaws, what are they? Why do you think they exist?

Knowing that something inside you is not quite right is the first step to changing or getting rid of it. First, however, we must admit there is a problem before we can start working on it. There is a reason we have those flaws, and we must do everything we can to rid ourselves of them.

Write the character flaws you see in yourself. Think about where they started and list ways to change or remove them from you.

NAME OF CHARACTER FLAW	FIRST BEGAN WHEN?	WHAT NEEDS TO TAKE PLACE TO REMOVE IT?

My Testimony

I can relate to Potiphar's wife because I knew many women, including me, who behaved in the same way. When I was a teenager, I, too, pursued things and people who were off-limits. One would think knowing they were not available would have stopped me, but it did not. Having a desire for something or someone unavailable can be devastating to the pursuer when she is rejected. However, the one thing I did not experience was rejection.

Living life in that manner was not how I was raised. Instead, I was taught not to covet others or their belongings. Eventually, I gave up pursuing what did not belong to me.

I rededicated my life to Christ, and I realized what I did was wrong. I repented and never looked back. I refused to be a hypocrite in the kingdom, so I had to come clean with God. Either I was for Christ 100 percent or I was for the world. I could not have them both. The appearance of other men no longer tempts me. I have eyes only for my husband. God has blessed me with an amazing husband, and he is the only one I desire to be with. I thank God for delivering and freeing me from that tumultuous lifestyle that almost had me bound.

Prayer

Father God, thank You for forgiving and delivering me from my deceitful ways. I have not always been the woman you called me to be. I have made some horrible mistakes. I made excuses for my actions and told myself it was okay. Lord, without your delivering power, I do not know where I would be right now. Thank You for creating in me a clean heart and renewing the right spirit within me. Thank you for changing me and taking everything out of me that is not like You. Thank You for blessing me with the husband You had for me and preparing me for him so that I could do what is right in Your eyes in this marriage. Lord, You are amazing. I love You, Lord! Thank You for always being here for me. It is in Your Son, Jesus's name, I pray, amen!

Notes

Chapter Ten
A LONGING DESIRE

Samson's Mother
JUDGES 13:3-5, 13-14, 22-24 (NASB)

³Then the angel of the Lord appeared to the woman, and said to her, "Behold now, you are barren and have borne no children, but you shall conceive and give birth to a son. ⁴"Now therefore, be careful not to drink wine or strong drink, nor eat any unclean thing. ⁵"For behold, you shall conceive and give birth to a son, and no razor shall come upon his head, for the boy shall be a Nazirite to God from the womb, and he shall begin to deliver Israel from the hands of the Philistines." ¹³So the angel of the Lord said to Manoah, "Let the woman pay attention all that I said. ¹⁴"She should not eat anything that comes from the vine nor drink wine or strong drink, nor eat any unclean thing; let her observe all that I commanded. ²²So Manoah said to his wife, "We shall surely die, for we have seen God." ²³But his wife said to him, "if the Lord had desired to kill us, He would not have accepted a burnt offering and a grain offering from our hands, nor would He have shown us all these things, nor would he have let us hear things like this at this time. ²⁴Then the woman gave birth to a son and named him Samson; and the child grew up and the Lord blessed him.

Her Story

Samson's mother was a godly, barren woman. She was adamant about obeying God, which was evident by her life choices. After the angel appeared before her and delivered a message from God, she went to her husband and delivered the same message to him. She knew God had a plan for the son she would birth, and she was not going to do anything to go against God's instructions.

> Do you find it difficult to adhere to God's instructions? If so, why is that? If not, how do you display such strength? Explain.

The angel of God appeared to Samson's mother again. She ran to get her husband so he could meet the angel. They both had questions as to how to raise their son. After she told her husband, Manoah, all that was spoken to her by the angel of God, Manoah prayed and asked God to teach them how to raise their son when he was born. Notice her husband said *when*, not *if* when asking what the boy's responsibilities would be. That question showed a tremendous amount of faith.

> Walking by faith can be hard to do at times. When God shows or speaks something to you, do you immediately believe or hesitantly proceed with caution?

> Has there ever been a time in your life when you or someone you know has had to walk by faith? What did that entail?

The angel spoke God's word to Samson's mother. She believed what she heard and told her husband. He took her word, prayed to God, and received another visit to answer any questions they had concerning the birth of their son.

When someone comes to us with a word from the Lord, we should always confer with God first before acting on what we've been told.

> Are you in the habit of taking others' words for your circumstances, or do you immediately talk to God about what you just received?

She did as she was instructed by the angel of God when she conceived. She gave birth to a healthy baby boy and named him Samson. The Lord blessed her son as he grew. However, he ended up straying from all that his parents taught him.

Although she made godly choices, there was no guarantee that her adult son would do the same. Samson's mother had no idea her son would go against God's command when he grew into adulthood.

> If you are raising a child, what are your expectations for that child? If your child does not live up to your expectations, explain how you would deal with their choices.

> If you have not raised a child but know someone who has, would you be willing to step in and give assistance or advice to that adult son or daughter based on your life experiences? Please explain how you would approach them and proceed with giving them advice.

Raising a child is challenging to say the least. Yet we all hope our children would grow up living for Christ, just as Samson's mother did.

However, the reality is, all we can do is set the foundation and keep praying. Once they become adults, they are no longer obligated to live according to our rules, beliefs, and guidance. We have to pray that the foundation set during their early childhood years was a solid one that will be embedded in their hearts for the rest of their lives.

Although we do not want to let our children go, we have to release them into the world and have faith that they will take God with them wherever they go.

God instructed Samson's mother to live by His instructions, and she did as He directed without wavering. However, once Samson became an adult, he was able to make his own decisions. Samson knew God did not want him to be unequally yoked, but that did not matter to him. He wanted what he wanted, and regardless of what his parents said, he was determined to have the Philistine woman who caught and kept his eye.

We cannot choose for our children. We can only guide them and pray they will continue to listen.

Give an example of a time you rebelled against God and your parents after you became an adult.

Application

List five attributes you see or saw in your child(ren).

1. _____
2. _____
3. _____
4. _____
5. _____

List five attributes you see or wish to see in them as adults.

1. _____
2. _____
3. _____
4. _____
5. _____

Are these attributes the same? If not, what changed?

Making godly choices can be a challenge for some. Whether it is related to our children or ourselves, it can still be tough. Of course, we all want to do what's right, but that isn't always the case when choosing what we feel is right and knowing what God says is right.

Give some examples of choosing between what you want to do and what God says to do.

WHAT I WANT TO DO	WHAT GOD WANTS ME TO DO

I AM EVERY WOMAN

My Testimony

I can honestly say that raising children is not an easy job. I have three daughters, and all of them are different, yet somehow the same. I raised two of them practically on my own. Their father and I divorced when the youngest was seven and the oldest was ten. Being a single mother was difficult, but that did not change how I raised them.

Early on, I was not raising them as a godly parent because I was not living the life of a Christian. However, because I was raised in the church, I knew the path God would have me guide them down. So I took them to church whenever I decided to go. Even though I did not obey all of God's instructions regarding the rearing of my girls, I still tried to instill godly principles in them. I wanted them to grow up serving and pleasing Him. My desire for them was to live a life that God would approve of. Although my life was reflective of the world at that time, I did not want theirs to be the same. It was not until I rededicated my life to Christ that I realized I had to step my game up with my two daughters, and I did precisely that.

Fast-forward to their youngest sister. Her father and I were both saved and living godly lives when she was born. She has lived in a Christian household all her life. Serving God every Sunday is a regular occurrence in her life. We want her to marry a believer in Jesus Christ, just as we wanted for my two oldest daughters. (By the way, both of their husbands are believers. Praise God!) All we can do now is wait and see if rearing her in a Christian household and teaching her about Jesus and His word will lead her to continue following Him as an adult. We can only hope and pray that she does.

We don't know which direction she will choose, but we are prayerful and hopeful that Christ will be Lord over her life, just as He is over the rest of our family. I have seen many parents raise their children according to God's word and end up like Samson. If this is you, don't give up and don't lose hope because, in the end, Samson came back to God. Keep the faith, and prayerfully your child will return to God as well. You have to believe that.

Prayer

Father God, thank You for teaching me how to be the parent You called me to be. Thank You for not allowing me to stay in a backslidden state. Thank You for writing Your words in the hearts of our children. We know that life would be even more difficult than it already is to navigate through without You. Lord, continue to guide us as parents. Keep our children covered in Your blood. We know that the devil out of hell cannot penetrate the blood of Jesus, and as long as they are covered in Your blood, we can rest and not worry. Thank You for hearing and answering my prayers. It is in Your Son, Jesus's name, I pray, amen!

Notes

Chapter Eleven
THE AVENGER

Jael
JUDGES 4:4–9, 17–22 (NASB)

⁴Now Deborah, a prophetess, the wife of Lappidoth, was judging Israel at that time. ⁵She used to sit under the palm tree of Deborah between Ramah and Bethel in the hill country of Ephraim; and the sons of Israel came up to her for judgment. ⁶Now she sent and summoned Barak the son of Abinoam from Kedesh-naphtali, and said to him, "Behold, the Lord, the God of Israel, has commanded, 'Go and march to Mount Tabor, and take with you ten thousand men from the sons of Naphtali and from the sons of Zebulun. ⁷I will draw out to you Sisera, the commander of Jabin's army, with his chariots and his many troops to the river Kishon, and I will give him into your hand.'" ⁸Then Barak said to her, "If you will go with me, then I will go; but if you will not go with me, I will not go."

⁹She said, "I will surely go with you; nevertheless, the honor shall not be yours on the journey that you are about to take, for the Lord will sell Sisera into the hands of a woman." ¹⁷Now Sisera fled away on foot to the tent of Jael the wife of Heber the Kenite, for there was peace between Jabin the king of Hazor and the house of Heber the Kenite. ¹⁸And Jael went out to meet Sisera, and said to him, "Turn aside, my master, turn aside to me! Do not be afraid." And he turned aside to her into the tent, and she covered him with a rug. ¹⁹And he said to her, "Please give me a little water to drink, for I am thirsty." So she opened a bottle of milk and gave him a drink; then she covered him. ²⁰And he said to her, "Stand in the doorway of the tent, and it shall

be if anyone comes and inquires of you, and says, 'Is there anyone here?' that you shall say, 'No.'" ²¹But Jael, Heber's wife, took a tent peg and seized a hammer in her hand, and went secretly to him and drove the peg into his temple, and it went through into the ground; for he was sound asleep and exhausted. So he died. ²²And behold, as Barak pursued Sisera, Jael came out to meet him and said to him, "Come, and I will show you the man whom you are seeking." And he entered with her, and behold Sisera was lying dead with the tent peg in his temple.

Her Story

God used Jael to avenge the Israelites from the hands of Jabin. He and his army had oppressed them for twenty years. Sisera, the commander of Jabin's army, played a significant role in ensuring the Israelites remained oppressed. Little did he know that his reign as commander was about to end. God's plan was activated when the Israelites cried out to God to free them from their oppressors. He used Jael to accomplish His plan. Because Jael's husband and Jabin were allies, Sisera believed he could trust her. He felt comfortable accepting her offer to come into her tent and rest. He was exhausted from being chased by Barak. When she told him not to be afraid, that should have been a sign that something was not quite right. Think about it, if Jael's husband, Heber, and Sisera's king, King Hazor, were friends, why would he be afraid? Certainly nothing would happen to him in the tent of his king's friend.

He had no idea he was walking into God's strategic plan of defeat. Jael was God's avenger who would lead Sisera to his death. The most unexpected person just happened to be a woman. He never suspected she would be the one to end his life. Had he known, he wouldn't have felt safe enough to enter her tent. Instead, she played the perfect role. Her ability to portray a humble, sweet, kind hostess who would protect him from Barak was all a part of God's divine setup to free His people from twenty years of oppression.

She saw an opportunity to save God's people and end their oppression. Therefore, when Sisera fell into a deep sleep, Jael killed him by driving a tent peg into his temple with a hammer.

Jael showed a great deal of tenacity and willingness to take a chance on something that could have gone wrong. During those times, the husbands were the ones who made decisions such as these. Jael's husband was not around, so she took it upon herself to complete the task and deliver Sisera's lifeless body to Barak and his soldiers.

> If others oppressed someone close to you, how would you handle it?

Jael chose to help the Israelites, which went against her husband's demands. The impetus to commit such an act had to come from God alone. She was not a naïve, easily manipulated woman. On the contrary, she proved to be a strong, confident woman who knew what she needed to do to become allies with God's chosen people. A decision needed to be made quickly, and in the absence of her husband, she did just that. Jael showed a great deal of strength.

Everyone knew God chose the Israelites, and at any given moment, God would set the course to save them once again. On her part, it was pretty smart to side with the victors who had the living God on their side. Now, she and her family were committed to a partnership with the Israelites.

> Put yourself in Jael's place. Would you have responded the same way? Why or why not?

Ultimately, Jael was doing the will of God. Deborah had prophesized to Barak that God would deliver Sisera into the hands of a woman, and that is precisely what happened. God is always in control. He uses ayone He chooses to achieve His plan. Jael unknowingly carried out God's will.

> Looking back over your life and examining all the acts you participated in, whether good or bad, do you think it was God's will? Why or why not?

Because Barak refused to obey God, He chose to use a woman. God always has someone readily available to bring His will to pass, whether the person knows it or not. Jael may not have known this was orchestrated by God, but God's will was accomplished through her.

> Has there ever been a time when you or someone you know was disobedient to God? How did that turn out for you or them?

Jael did the unthinkable and acted without her husband's consent. We do not know if they were of one accord or not, but what we do know is women did not take matters into their own hands during those times. Heber left her alone, so he must have had enough confidence in her to handle anything that came her way during his absence.

> Discuss your relationship. Are you all of one accord or not? Explain.

> Is there enough trust in both parties for you to make a decision without his knowledge that would affect your family and life forever? Please explain.

> If Jael and her husband were not on the same page, do you think she would have acted so boldly, without hesitation? Why or why not?

Application

We all know that God is in control, and when He has a plan, it will happen. God may be calling you to participate in His plan, and you may not know it. There is usually an unction deep within you to move forward or away from something when God is nudging you to a different place.

He uses many different people and things to speak to us.

Are you in a place to hear from God?

Sometimes we feel the need to proceed in unknown territory, but we hesitate because we don't know what the outcome will be. Knowing God's voice is extremely important. Although Jael did not know that God chose to use her for His children, we should know.

How do you know it is God leading you?

| Discuss your willingness to do what God is calling you to do.

Name some actions you would be willing to participate in to save your family. Then list the ones you would never take part in, regardless of what was at stake.

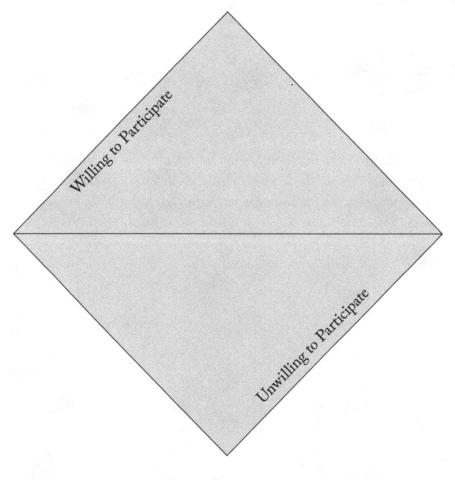

My Testimony

As I examine my life, I think about all I've endured over the years. Now I see how God used me to accomplish His plan. My exposure to criminal activities and knowing the outcome of continuing down that path led me to get on the right track. Had I not experienced all I did, I cannot say I would be doing the work of the Lord today.

God led Sisera to Jael's tent, and because of His plan for the Israelites, she did exactly what He intended her to. There have been times when God led someone to me, and I failed to do what I knew in my heart I should have done. By not being obedient, I delayed my blessing and endured many setbacks. My disobedience may have delayed the blessings of others as well. Unlike Jael, I knew God intended to use me. However, I did not want to obey at the time. Over the years, I learned that the people God chooses to use to accomplish His plan are already in place.

The way God strategically planned everything out without Jael's knowledge made me wonder if I would have ignored Him or refused to be a willing participant had He done the same to me. Jael boldly and willingly took Sisera's life, and that brave act ended the oppression of the Israelites. I cannot say for sure what I would have done, but I will say that whenever I've taken a different route than what was in my heart to choose, the outcome was always unfavorable. It was not until I got tired of falling on my face and losing all the time that I decided to follow what was in my heart. This is when I would pray and ask God, "Lord, what is it that You would have me do? How do you want me to proceed?" It is not that I did not know God was leading me in a specific direction or taking part in a particular event or activity. I just wanted to do things my way. Epic failure!

Well, over the years, after failing and remaining in one place for many years, I have learned that God's way is the best and not to fight against what I know God is instructing me to do. The consequences of disobeying are not worth enduring.

Prayer

Father God, thank You for giving me chance after chance to get it right. I disobeyed You many times, and You never gave up on me. You always made sure I got back on track. I now know that no matter what, Your plans will always prevail. I can *never* win up against You. My will to do what I want has gotten me in a great deal of trouble and brought about numerous setbacks. Learning to listen to Your voice and do what I know You are instructing me to do has been a journey in itself. Unlike Jael, I knew You were calling me to participate in Your plan, and many times I was disobedient. Thank You for not leaving me in that state. I repented. You forgave me and gave me another chance to get it right. Lord, I thank You for that. Thank You for choosing me to be a part of what You are doing in this season of my life. It is in Your Son, Jesus's name, I pray, amen!

Notes

Chapter Twelve
THE POWER OF PAGANISM: SOLOMON'S PAGAN WIVES

KINGS 11:1-6 (HCSB)

¹King Solomon loved many foreign women in addition to Pharaoh's daughter: Moabite, Ammonite, Edomite, Sidonian, and Hittite women ²from the nations that the Lord had told the Israelites about, "Do not intermarry with them, and they must not intermarry with you because they will turn you away from Me to their gods." Solomon was deeply attached to these women and loved them. ³He had 700 wives who were princesses and 300 concubines, and they turned his heart away from the Lord. ⁴When Solomon was old, his wives seduced him to follow other gods. He was not completely devoted to Yahweh his God, as his father David had been. ⁵Solomon followed Ashtoreth, the goddess of the Sidonians, and Milcom, the detestable idol of the Ammonites. ⁶Solomon did what was evil in the Lord's sight, and unlike his father David, he did not completely follow Yahweh.

Her Story

Solomon's wives were the very women God warned him not to marry. They did not serve Yahweh (God). They served their gods instead. The ways of these women would eventually contaminate the ways of a godly man.

Women have the power to influence whatever or whoever they choose. But if they are not careful, their power can be used to destroy.

He married seven hundred princesses and three hundred concubines. Because they were not believers, their behaviors were a reflection of the world in which they lived. They followed after pagan gods. One, in particular, was Ashtoreth. She was the goddess of the Sidonians.

The pagan wives had a power that no man could match or resist. Anytime a woman can turn one from God, her ability to override that human will is revealed. During those days, God forbade His people to intermarry with unbelievers. Even today, He tells us not to be unequally yoked with unbelievers. But for some reason, some of us find ourselves in the same predicament as Solomon, desiring those God instructed us to stay away from.

The pagan wives are great examples of how much power women have over their families, mainly their husbands. Women set the standard in many households. This includes the grandmothers, mothers, daughters, sisters, and aunts.

> Name one influence you know you have over the man in your life. Why do you think you hold that power?

Just as the pagan wives walked in their power and used it to their advantage, we can do the same. But we must remember that our power could be used as either a constructive or destructive tool.

The Bible displays women's influences in many different forms, both negative and positive.

Many of the negative influences throughout the Bible did not end well. Here are a few who faced dire consequences:

- Eve influenced Adam to eat the forbidden fruit.
- Potiphar's wife used lies and deceit to influence him to throw Joseph, an innocent man, in jail.
- Herod's wife used her influence to behead John the Baptist. She was an opportunist. She saw an opportunity to get rid of the man she hated and used it to get him killed.
- Jezebel used her influence on her husband, King Ahab, and persuaded him to worship Baal.

Influence can be detrimental to your life if not used responsibly. This is a fact that many women should consider before divulging their influential powers.

To show how positive influences have a better outcome, five women demonstrated using their power positively.

- Pilot's wife influenced him not to have a hand in crucifying Jesus. He listened.
- Ruth used wisdom to influence Boaz. She won his heart.
- Esther used her influence to save her people. They were saved.
- Proverbs 31 woman: a wise woman builds her house. She lives life in a manner that will benefit not only herself but her family as well.
- Hannah used her influence to turn God, not man. She was barren. She cried out, worshipped God, and said, "Lord, remember me!" And God remembered her, based upon her request, and she became pregnant.

God's plan will always lend a favorable outcome.

> Who can you relate to, the positive influencer or the negative one? Why?

As wives, they were not just some bystanders or spectators in Solomon's home. We, as women, are the same. Many of us are not bystanders or spectators in our homes. We have power.

Just as the pagan wives misled Solomon, we can do the same. We can deceive our husbands and family. Even if you're not married, there are other men in your family or inner circle with whom you have a significant influence.

If the pagan wives would've positively used their power, the outcome would've been different. Instead, seduction was their greatest weapon. There's something about the power of seduction when it comes to getting men to do what women want them to.

They used seduction as a way to influence Solomon to turn to their gods. They did not force him. They influenced him. There is a difference.

We cannot make anyone do anything. But we can influence or persuade them, depending on the method we choose to use.

> What methods have you used to persuade someone to do what you wanted?

> What is your greatest weapon when it comes to persuasion?

A woman who recognizes her influence can use it to build or tear down. Once she acknowledges what she can do, it is about balance and how she uses it; being responsible and accountable are critical factors in this decision.

The pagan wives did not have a God to be accountable to. So they worshipped idols, not a living God as we do. Whenever idols rule over your life, your decisions will always sway negatively.

> What are some idols in your life that control you?

We have the power to do what we want. Remember Adam? He knew what God said, but Eve enticed him, which caused him to disobey God. He chose his wife's suggestion over God's command.

> What kind of influence do you have? How are you using this influence?

The pagan wives were selfish, which led them to display selfish ambitions. They only wanted to please themselves. However, they did not consider the consequences of being selfish, and if they did, it did not matter because they still influenced Solomon to commit an act that went against everything God told him.

> Take a step back and look at your life. Do you see any selfish ambitions lurking in your life? If so, what are they?

Application

Recognizing the gift we have and being responsible for it is imperative to living a life pleasing to God. Just like Ruth used wisdom and humility to influence Boaz by following Naomi's instructions, we can do the same by following God's instructions. Influence expresses itself in many different ways. Some women use trickery to get what they want, just like Tamar did when she dressed like a prostitute and tricked Judah into sleeping with her so she could conceive. On the other hand, some of us use fear and intimidation, as Jezebel did.

We, as women, have a responsibility to use our influences for good and not evil. Even if we are correct when we use our power, we should still use it responsibly.

> What was the outcome of you using your power for the greater good/evil?

There are numerous scenarios of how families are coming together and falling apart, all from how women use their influences. This is not blaming women. It is showing that a woman's power can make a difference. It is like throwing the rock and hiding your hand. Yes, Adam ate the apple, but he would have never touched it had it not been for the influence of Eve. There is a great deal of danger when a woman uses her power for her benefit and not her family's. It takes strength and maturity on the part of the woman not to use her power for only her good.

How has your influence benefited you, your family, or both?

Think about all the influential power you have stored up inside you. What are some of the pros and cons you see?

PROS OF MY INFLUENCE	CONS OF MY INFLUENCE

My Testimony

Throughout my life, I have used my power of influence for both good and evil. I have been highly selfish in many situations. At one point, it was all about me. I did not care who I hurt as long as I got what I wanted. I was a manipulator, user, conwoman, and to top it all off, I was arrogant about all I could accomplish with my power. I sat around thinking of ways to draw guys in, only to give them a piece of their own medicine. Because I saw how men used women, I wanted nothing more than to do the same. Because of my intellect, I was able to woo them with my words.

After a while, I began using other tactics to get what I wanted. Yes, it worked every time. I had the mental and physical power to overcome any obstacle I faced when I was out to win. I was not humble like Esther. I was not wise like Ruth. I was more like Tamar—sneaky and conniving. I thrived on being deceitful, like Potiphar's wife. As you can tell, I was more like the negative influences. It was not until I rededicated my life to Christ that I began using my power for the greater good.

Through all that I did, I always thought about what would happen if I remained that way. Then, I had my first daughter at nineteen. Because of her, there was always a part of me that considered how my actions would affect her in the long run. Before I had her, I did not care what outcomes my efforts would bring. Having her brought a whole new perspective to how I used my power of influence. I knew I needed to keep her out of harm's way, so I became more cautious of what, how, and who I used my influence with. I honestly believe God allowed me to get pregnant at that age to slow me down. It worked to a certain extent.

If God had not saved me from me, there's no telling where I would be right now. As I examine my past, I realize how catastrophic it could have been for my child and me. Knowing what I know now, I would choose differently were I given the opportunity to do so. I would be the positive influence instead of the negative one.

Prayer

Father God, thank You for teaching me how to use my power of influence for the greater good. As I look back over my life and all that I have done, I am so grateful to You for not only sparing my life but for saving me from myself. There are other women out there using their influence for evil. Turn their hearts to You so their impact will be used for good. Take away the selfishness some are living with and replace it with compassion and love for others. Knowing that my life could have taken a turn for the worst had I continued down my path, I now see things from a different perspective. You opened my eyes and let me see that if I used my influence for good, I could help so many other women turn their lives around as well. Thank You, Lord, for not giving up on me. Thank You for never leaving me. Lord, I am forever grateful to You.

It is in Your Son, Jesus's name I pray, amen!

Notes

Encouraging Words

While writing, *I am Every Woman,* the similarities in the lives of these biblical women paralyzed me as I compared their problems and mishaps to mine. It was as if I were looking in a mirror.

This book details a part of who I was, and it has allowed me to share my innermost feelings and thoughts with others.

As women, we deal with a plethora of issues, both internal and external. Without the proper guidance, many of us would be lost. I found solace in writing *I am Every Woman* because it allowed me to dig deep within myself and address many issues I thought no longer existed.

I have learned to kill the root of my problems so that I can heal and grow. However, if we do not destroy the core, the problem will continue to resurface into something greater than before.

Many of my issues stemmed from childhood. It was not until I became an adult that I was able to face them head-on. With the help of God, I was able to overcome.

We all have our battles. Some can handle them on their own, whereas others cannot. Our attitudes toward our obstacles and challenges will always determine the outcome.

I pray that the stories and my testimonies help you work through your issues as they arise. There may be someone you know facing the same obstacles that these women and I have encountered. If so, I pray that you can help them conquer their problems by using this book as well.

CPSIA information can be obtained
at www.ICGtesting.com
Printed in the USA
BVHW040712011022
648466BV00004B/57